Words Carry Power

Speak Words of Faith

Sharron Downs

Words Carry Power: Speak Words of Faith
Second Edition
By Author Sharron Downs
Published by Sharron Downs
Paperback ISBN: 9798320978697
Email: Sharron@Sharrondowns.info
Website: sharrondowns.info

Copyright © 2024

Contents

- Journal Notes

Book Dedication

This book is for anyone in need of change in their life. Change will take place starting with the words you speak. Speak life with your words. End your self sabotage.

Introduction

Words are extremely powerful and meaningful.

We need to speak only what you want things to be. Do not say anything you do not mean. Make sure to speak positive words daily. End negativity in your life.

Spoken positive words from the word of God will change your faith, life and show you a new way to live. Be blessed and continue to believe the importance of the spoken word. Believe the impossible and watch God perform a miracle in your life all because of the words you speak with faith.

How should we use words?

Well, here are some ways to speak words of faith on a daily basis.

Why should you care about how to use words? Well, Words carry power. What do I mean? Well, the bible says Life and Death are in the power of the tongue. See three different translations of the Bible for clarity and the meaning behind words.

Scripture: *"Death and life are in the power of the tongue: And they that love it shall eat the fruit thereof."* **Proverbs 18:21 KJV**

"Your words are so powerful that they will kill or give life, and the talkative person will reap the consequences." **Proverbs 18:21 TPT**

"Words kill, words give life; they're either poison or fruit—you choose." **Proverbs 18:21 MSG**

When you choose to speak life with your words, whether on yourself or on others, make sure they are words of faith and positive.

When you speak positive words, affirmations and decrees as the Lord has spoken to us in the Bible, your life will change.

Words were used to create the earth. God spoke a word, the Bible tells us in the **scripture**: *"In the beginning God (Elohim) created [by forming from nothing] the heavens and the earth. And God said, "Let there be light"; and there was light. And God called the light day, and the darkness He called night. And there was* *evening and there was morning, one day. And God said, "Let there be an expanse [of the sky] in the midst of the waters, and let it separate the waters [below the expanse] from the waters [above the expanse]." Then God said, "Let the waters below the heavens be gathered into one place [of standing, pooling together], and let the dry land appear"; and it was so. God called the dry land earth, and the gathering of the waters He called seas; and God saw that this was good (pleasing, useful) and He affirmed and sustained it. So God said, "Let the earth sprout [tender] vegetation, plants yielding seed, and fruit trees bearing fruit according to (limited to, consistent with) their kind, whose seed is in them upon the earth"; and it was so. Then*

God said, "Let there be
light-bearers (sun, moon, stars) in
the expanse of the heavens to
separate the day from the night,
and let them be useful for signs
(tokens) [of God's provident care],
and for marking seasons, days,
and years; Then God said, "Let the
waters swarm and abundantly
produce living creatures, and let
birds soar above the earth in the
open expanse of the heavens."
And God blessed them, saying,
"Be fruitful, multiply, and fill the
waters in the seas, and let birds
multiply on the earth." Then God
said, "Let Us (Father, Son, Holy
Spirit) make man in Our image,
according to Our likeness [not
physical, but a spiritual
personality and moral likeness];
and let them have complete
authority over the fish of the sea,

the birds of the air, the cattle, and over the entire earth, and over everything that creeps and crawls on the earth." So God created man in His own image, in the image and likeness of God He created him; male and female He created them. And God blessed them [granting them certain authority] and said to them, "Be fruitful, multiply, and fill the earth, and subjugate it [putting it under your power]; and rule over (dominate) the fish of the sea, the birds of the air, and every living thing that moves upon the earth." God saw everything that He had made, and behold, it was very good and He validated it completely. And there was evening and there was morning, a sixth day." **Genesis 1:1, 3, 5-6, 9-11, 14, 20, 22, 26-28, 31 AMP**

If God can speak WORDS and
things happen then why can't we
as His children? We are made in
God's image just like scripture
says. We have been taught to say
silent prayers and do not say
things out loud (deception). God
spoke out loud. Why? God created
everything with powerful words of
faith. We can do the same.

Words of Faith. **Scripture** says,
*"But how can people call for help
if they don't know who to trust?
And how can they know who to
trust if they haven't heard of the
One who can be trusted? And
how can they hear if nobody tells
them? And how is anyone going
to tell them, unless someone is
sent to do it? That's why Scripture
exclaims, A sight to take your
breath away! Grand processions
of people telling all the good*

things of God! But not everybody is ready for this, ready to see and hear and act. Isaiah asked what we all ask at one time or another: "Does anyone care, God? Is anyone listening and believing a word of it?" The point is: Before you trust, you have to listen. But unless Christ's Word is preached, there's nothing to listen to." **Romans 10:14-17 MSG**

Also, **scripture** says: *"So then faith cometh by hearing, and hearing by the word of God."* **Romans 10:17 KJV**

Speak and call things into existence just like God. We are called to be imitators of God.

Scripture says, *"Therefore become imitators of God [copy Him and follow His example], as well-beloved children [imitate*

their father]; and walk continually in love [that is, value one another—practice empathy and compassion, unselfishly seeking the best for others], just as Christ also loved you and gave Himself up for us, an offering and sacrifice to God [slain for you, so that it became] a sweet fragrance."
Ephesians 5:1-2 AMP

Everytime you speak, listen to the words you are speaking. Make a conscious effort to only say what you expect to see and for God to make happen in your life.

Scripture: *"As for me, this is my covenant with them, saith the LORD; My spirit that is upon thee, and my words which I have put in thy mouth, shall not depart out of thy mouth, nor out of the mouth of thy seed, nor out of the mouth* *of thy seed's seed, saith the LORD, from henceforth and for ever."* **Isaiah 59:21 KJV**

"Believest thou not that I am in the Father, and the Father in me? the words that I speak unto you I speak not of myself: but the Father that dwelleth in me, he doeth the works." **John 14:10 KJV**

Make a conscious effort to have the determination and strive to only allow positivity around you. Do not accept negative words to be spoken to you or over you. End all self sabotage today.

Scripture says: *""The Holy Spirit is the one who gives life, that which is of the natural realm is of no help. The words I speak to you are Spirit and life. But there are still some of you who won't believe.""* **John 6:63 TPT**

Only agree to what the word of God says. You should refuse to accept anything less. You are chosen and unique, now is the time to speak like a man and woman of faith, God's way.

Scripture says: *"But Jesus replied, "It is written and forever remains written, 'Man shall not live by bread alone, but by every word that comes out of the mouth of God.'""* **Matthew 4:4 AMP**

Let's look more into scripture and see how this process works for us.

Scripture says: *"I assure you and most solemnly say to you, whoever says to this mountain, 'Be lifted up and thrown into the sea!' and does not doubt in his heart [in God's unlimited power], but believes that what he says is going to take place, it will be done*

for him [in accordance with God's will]. For this reason I am telling you, whatever things you ask for in prayer [in accordance with God's will], believe [with confident trust] that you have received them, and they will be given to you. Whenever you stand praying, if you have anything against anyone, forgive him [drop the issue, let it go], so that your Father who is in heaven will also forgive you your transgressions and wrongdoings [against Him and others]. [But if you do not forgive, neither will your Father in heaven forgive your transgressions."]"
Mark 11:23-26 AMP

What powerful words will you say daily as affirmations over yourself after reading the scriptures and content from above?

Write them below - hold yourself accountable.

What powerful words will you say
daily as decrees over yourself after
reading the scriptures and
content from above?

**Write them below - hold yourself
accountable.**

____

____

____

____

____

____

____

____

____

____

Illustration of Ways To Improve The Words We Speak

Excerpts from my book "Change Your World With Words."

Words are Powerful. What do I mean? Well, I mean you can speak "positive words" or you can speak "negative words," when you are having a conversation with others or even when you say something to yourself.

Here are a few examples, "man, my feet are killing me." or "you make me sick" or "you are stupid" or "I hate your guts" another is "I'm dying to go to that concert" last example is when you hear a joke and say, "aww you're killing me" well you really don't mean those phrases.

You have been saying these phrases for so long, you don't even realize what you are saying. These are not phrases you want to choose to say.

How often do we say things we do not mean only because we have been saying them either all our lives or just happen to pick it up from someone of influence.

These are negative words and we definitely do not need to say these words, not even as a joke. When this happens please make sure to cancel those words immediately and say a blessing over yourself and not a curse.

Positive words can and will create your world and atmosphere. You will ultimately have what you say. Choose to speak words wisely. I can definitely say this has happened to me in the past and I no longer use these "phrases" or any like those I have mentioned.

Another example of positive and negative words are found in certain songs you sing and phrases you repeat. Also, the things you see on television, read on social media, may have a negative impact and we have to be extremely careful of what we are saying and what words you allow to be spoken over you.

"Garbage" (garbage words are like bad words) these should not be allowed to enter your ear gates nor your eye gates. Garbage in garbage out is a phrase said very often. Garbage does not go out quickly, it lingers and may spread into negativity. Garbage words are hard to get rid of along with these negative behaviors.

We have to want to change. We need to make a conscious effort to change the words we speak. This means certain movies are not good for you either.

If the spoken word causes you to act negative and be negative they are not good. You will probably hear me say words have power several times throughout this book. Words carry power. I definitely want you to have a life of abundance and peace which can be created through your words.

The words we speak can definitely

change your world for good or bad. If God can speak a world into existence then what would make you think words do not carry power. We are created in the image of God so let's act like it and speak positive words and pay closer attention to what we are saying.

Speak Words of Faith, Hope and Love

Start a new life now with positive words and affirmations. Speak words of faith, positive words, affirmations and decrees. It works according to your faith.

Make every effort to cancel all negative words as soon as you hear them spoken out of your mouth. Also, do not speak badly about others, especially your spouse, children or family. Always speak encouragement and what you expect them to become. Remember our words carry power. I can think of several ethnicities which speak to their children while in the womb and throughout their lives; "you will be a doctor someday, you are precious, you will make something of yourself, your my lawyer, engineer and top of your class child." They say this daily and the child starts to believe it. They speak words of faith and speak into existence what they want from their children. Then we have other ethnicities which do the opposite, they say things like, " you will never amount to anything, you are just like your father, good for nothing, you are stupid, dumb, no one wants you, look at you why can't you be like so and so, I hate that I had you." How should children feel when they hear this shouted at them all the time? Not so good right. Culture differences are real and we need to break this curse. It can start with you today. Cancel all negative things words spoken over you, your children and grandchildren and decree what God says about them.

They are made in the image of God, blessed, highly favored, anointed to prosper.

Therefore, from this day forward, **_"Fall out of agreement with anything that is not according to the word of God. Stop saying bad words, curse words, cuss words and eliminate bad habits."_**

What are some things you can do
and start to say differently, to help
you speak positively?

What will be your daily routine to
bring positive Words into your
day?

Words to Speak over your health

Here is something to think about. Picture this, most people go to the doctor, hospital, dentist or a specialist they tend to believe and take the advice and diagnosis of their clinician.

Well, if your doctor is God and you believe the word that by Jesus stripes you are healed, then why are you sick and accept the Words spoken to you from the doctor? Most doctors are "practicing medicine". They don't know what to do for you until you *tell* (spoken words) them the symptoms and family history.

Well, here is something to ponder.

Let's say, you have a healthy family, no sickness or disease runs in your family on either side. You do not put a check mark on the paperwork from any category. You say, I'm here for a physical for my insurance. Well, they have nothing to go on or compare you to. They take blood, check weight, blood pressure, listen to your heart, take pulse, ask if you take medication, ask if you have pain etc. Well, you are now healthy, they found nothing. The pharmacy will not receive any funding from you. The insurance company will just have a statement saying you were there. No worries right. All is well. That's it. No follow up. No one comes to say see you in six to twelve months, the end. So get dressed and leave.

Now, let's say you go for the same physical and say, you have problems sleeping, feel tired, feel pain in your neck or back occasionally and want to lose weight. The clinician recommends you see a specialist in each of those areas. Prescribe medication according to your symptoms. Now you really have issues because the medication is causing you to have problems with areas that were fine before you told (spoken words) the doctor a few things going on with you.

Now, the nurse prints a list of things from the internet with your symptoms. Then it suggests medication, then specialists, more doctors visits and soon you start to believe what they told you. Now you just stepped out of faith into the world system and you believe you have what they said, no second opinion or anything. You believe it because they are supposed to be experts. Well, the Bible you said you believe in was a good expert for you before coming to the doctor. Now the process you believed in is broken. Your faith has left you. You have signed up with the world system. The visit did not go as planned. Your words have been spoken and now, you have changed your life.

Why does this happen? Could the symptoms be a result of what you ate, not enough water, coffee or caffeine prior to your doctor visit. Could it be that you stayed up late watching television and feel tired? None of these factors were addressed and you are now on medication, taking sleep aids and now your body feels sluggish, you have falls, and start a downward spiral. All from what you. "said" the words you spoke.

God's word is medicine to your soul. **Scripture**: "Pleasant words are as an honeycomb, Sweet to the soul, and health to the bones." **Proverbs 16:24 KJV**

Scripture: "When they are sick, lying upon their bed of suffering, God will restore them. He will raise them up again and restore them back to health." Psalms 41:3 TPT

Scripture: "Hundreds of sick people were lying under the covered porches—the paralyzed, the blind, and the crippled—all of them waiting for their healing. For an angel of God periodically descended into the pool to stir the waters, and the first one who stepped into the pool after the waters swirled would instantly be healed. Among the many sick people lying there was a man who had been disabled for thirty-eight years. When Jesus saw him lying there, he knew that the man had been crippled for a long time. Jesus said to him, "Do you truly long to be well?" The sick man answered, "Sir, there's no way I can get healed, for I have no one to lower me into the water when the angel comes. As soon as I try to crawl to the edge of the pool, someone else jumps in ahead of me." Jesus said to him, "Stand up! Pick up your sleeping mat and you will walk!" Immediately he stood up—he was healed! So he rolled up his mat and

walked again! Now Jesus worked this miracle on the Sabbath."
John 5:3-9 TPT

Take it daily, eat healthy, speak life over yourself, tell yourself what God says about you, ask God what to do; do not agree with sickness and disease but expect healing, eat better, drink more water, get more exercise and rest, you will be healthy again. This is something few people do. Why? They do not know anything about this type of faith and how words which you speak when mixed with faith can work. This is also allowing the body God made to heal itself. This is trusting God in every area of your life.

Before you say this is crazy, what are you talking about? Just think

about what I have written and start
to pay close attention to the next
symptom or doctor visit. Think
about this scenario in the scripture.

Scripture: "And when he was come
into the house, the blind men came
to him: and Jesus saith unto them,
Believe ye that I am able to do this?
They said unto him, Yea, Lord. Then
touched he their eyes, saying,
According to your faith be it unto
you. And their eyes were opened;
and Jesus straitly charged them,
saying, See that no man know it.
But they, when they were departed,
spread abroad his fame in all that
country. As they went out, behold,
they brought to him a dumb man
possessed with a devil. And when
the devil was cast out, the dumb
spake: and the multitudes
marvelled, saying, It was never so

seen in Israel." **Matthew 9:28-33 KJV**

Here are a few **scriptures** to read and meditate on.

"The centurion answered and said, Lord, I am not worthy that thou shouldest come under my roof: but speak the word only, and my servant shall be healed." **Matthew 8:8 KJV**

"When you speak healing words, you offer others fruit from the tree of life. But unhealthy, negative words do nothing but crush their hopes." **Proverbs 15:4 TPT**

"Now my body is sick. My health is totally broken because of your anger, and it's all due to my sins!" **Psalms 38:3 TPT**

"For the time is coming when they will no longer listen and respond to the healing words of truth because they will become selfish and proud. They will seek out teachers with soothing words that line up with their desires, saying just what they want to hear." **2 Timothy 4:3 TPT**

"O Lord, help me again! Keep showing me such mercy. For I am in anguish, always in tears, and I'm worn out with weeping. I'm becoming old because of grief; my health is broken." **Psalms 31:9 TPT**

"But if anyone spreads false teaching that does not agree with the healthy instruction of our Lord Jesus, teaching others that holy awe of God is not important, then they prove they know nothing at all!

It's obvious they don't value or hold dear the healing words of our Lord Jesus Christ." **1 Timothy 6:3 TPT**

"For I am the LORD: I will speak, and the word that I shall speak shall come to pass; it shall be no more prolonged: for in your days, O rebellious house, will I say the word, and will perform it, saith the Lord GOD." **Ezekiel 12:25 KJV**

The words you speak carry meaning, power, faith, action, boldness, courage and strength. Start to use the power that's on the inside of your body as a child of God. Say, do and live differently with the words you speak.

Scriptures to meditate

"But those who don't love me will not obey my words. The Father did not send me to speak my own revelation, but the words of my Father." *John 14:24 TPT*

"Let no corrupt communication proceed out of your mouth, but that which is good to the use of edifying, that it may minister grace unto the hearers." *Ephesians 4:29 KJV*

"The teachings of the righteous are loaded with wisdom, but the words of the evil ones are crooked and perverse." *Proverbs 10:31 TPT*

"A final word: Be strong in the Lord and in his mighty power."
Ephesians 6:10 NLT

"Reckless words are like the thrusts of a sword, cutting remarks meant to stab and to hurt. But the words of the wise soothe and heal."
Proverbs 12:18 TPT

"Let the words of my mouth, and the meditation of my heart, be acceptable in thy sight, O LORD, my strength, and my redeemer." **Psalm 19:14 KJV**

"Out of the same mouth proceedeth blessing and cursing. My brethren, these things ought not so to be." **James 3:10 KJV**

"So here's what I want you to do, God helping you: Take your

everyday, ordinary life—your
sleeping, eating, going-to-work,
and walking-around life—and place
it before God as an offering.
Embracing what God does for you
is the best thing you can do for him.
Don't become so well-adjusted to
your culture that you fit into it
without even thinking. Instead, fix
your attention on God. You'll be
changed from the inside out.
Readily recognize what he wants
from you, and quickly respond to it.
Unlike the culture around you,
always dragging you down to its
level of immaturity, God brings the
best out of you, develops
well-formed maturity in you."
Romans 12:1-2 MSG

"In the beginning [before all time]
was the Word (Christ), and the
Word was with God, and the Word

was God Himself. He was [continually existing] in the beginning [co-eternally] with God. All things were made and came into existence through Him; and without Him not even one thing was made that has come into being. In Him was life [and the power to bestow life], and the life was the Light of men. The Light shines on in the darkness, and the darkness did not understand it or overpower it or appropriate it or absorb it [and is unreceptive to it]." *John 1:1-5 AMP*

"We have the same Spirit of faith that is described in the Scriptures when it says, "First I believed, then I spoke in faith." So we also first believe then speak in faith." *2 Corinthians 4:13 TPT*

"Put on salvation as your helmet, and take the sword of the Spirit, which is the word of God." **Ephesians 6:17 NLT**

"But be ye doers of the word, and not hearers only, deceiving your own selves." **James 1:22 KJV**

"Sharing words of wisdom is satisfying to your inner being. It encourages you to know that you've changed someone else's life." **Proverbs 18:20 TPT**

"The words of a wise person are gracious. The talk of a fool self-destructs— He starts out talking nonsense And ends up spouting insanity and evil." **Ecclesiastes 10:12-13 MSG**

"The mouth of a good person is a deep, life-giving well, but the mouth of the wicked is a dark cave of abuse." **Proverbs 10:11 MSG**

"The teachings of the righteous are loaded with wisdom, but the words of the evil ones are crooked and perverse. Words that bring delight pour from the lips of the godly, but the words of the wicked are duplicitous." **Proverbs 10:31-32 TPT**

"When we tell you these things, we do not use words that come from human wisdom. Instead, we speak words given to us by the Spirit, using the Spirit's words to explain spiritual truths." **1 Corinthians 2:13 NLT**

"Even when it seems I'm surrounded by many liars and my

own fears, and though I'm hurting in my suffering and trauma, I still stay faithful to God and speak words of faith." **Psalms 116:10-11 TPT**

"The words of his mouth were smoother than butter, but war was in his heart: His words were softer than oil, yet were they drawn swords." **Psalm 55:21 KJV**

"His words were smooth and charming. Yet his heart was disloyal and full of hatred— his words soft as silk while all the time scheming my demise. So here's what I've learned through it all: Leave all your cares and anxieties at the feet of the Lord, and measureless grace will strengthen you. He will watch over his devoted lovers, never letting them slip or be overthrown. He will send all my enemies to the pit of destruction. Murderers, liars, and betrayers will face an untimely death. My life's hope and trust is in you, and you'll never fail to rescue me!" **Psalms 55:21-23 TPT**

 "Your tongue devises destruction, Like a sharp razor, working deceitfully. You love evil more than good, Lying rather than speaking righteousness. Selah You love all devouring words, You deceitful tongue." **Psalms 52:2-4 NKJV**

"When you speak healing words, you offer others fruit from the tree of life. But unhealthy, negative words do nothing but crush their hopes." **Proverbs 15:4 TPT**

"For this cause also thank we God without ceasing, because, when ye received the word of God which ye heard of us, ye received it not as the word of men, but as it is in truth, the word of God, which effectually worketh also in you that believe." *1 Thessalonians 2:13 KJV*

"So how do we fit what we know of Abraham, our first father in the faith, into this new way of looking at things? If Abraham, by what he did for God, got God to approve him, he could certainly have taken credit for it. But the story we're given is a God-story, not an Abraham-story. What we read in Scripture is, "Abraham entered into what God was doing for him, and that was the turning point. He trusted God to set him right instead of trying to be right on his own."" *Romans 4:1-3 MSG*

"Words of wisdom flow from the one with true discernment. But to the heartless, words of wisdom become like rods beating their backside." **Proverbs 10:13 TPT**

"I speak with all sincerity; I speak the truth." **Job 33:3 NLT**

"The confidence of my calling enables me to overcome every difficulty without shame, for I have an intimate revelation of this God. And my faith in him convinces me that he is more than able to keep all that I've placed in his hands safe and secure until the fullness of his appearing. Allow the healing words you've heard from me to live in you and make them a model for life as your faith and love for the Anointed One grows even more. Guard well this incomparable treasure by the

Spirit of Holiness living within you."
2 Timothy 1:12-14 TPT

What are some things you want to do differently?

What are some scriptures you feel will help you?

DAILY AFFIRMATIONS

I AM RELYING ON GOD DAILY

I AM LIVING A LONG HEALTHY LIFE

I AM A CHILD OF THE LIVING GOD

I AM STRONG

I AM GROOMED FOR THIS MOMENT

I AM CAPABLE

I AM ALWAYS LISTENING FOR GOD'S VOICE

I AM NEVER EMBARRASSED

I AM ENERGY

I AM POWER

I AM STRENGTH

I AM WELL AND WHOLE IN EVERY PART OF MY BODY

I AM WELL AND BLESSED

I AM HEALED

I AM LIVING A LONG SATISFIED LIFE

I AM TO BE CELEBRATED

I AM DETERMINED TO SUCCEED

I AM SPEAKING WORDS OF FAITH

I AM ALLOWING GOD TO LEAD ME
DAILY

I AM NO LONGER LIVING IN FEAR

I AM IN LOVE WITH GOD

I AM HAPPY

I AM ENOUGH

I AM HEALTHY

I AM PROSPEROUS AND IN GOOD
HEALTH

I AM THE WORKMANSHIP OF GOD

I AM BLESSED WITH ALL SPIRITUAL
BLESSINGS

I AM WEALTHY

I AM ANOINTED TO PROSPER

I AM WALKING BY FAITH

I AM SEEKING WISDOM FROM ONLY
GOD

I AM LED BY MY FAITH IN GOD

I AM NO LONGER LIVING WITH
ANGER

I AM COMPLETE

I AM NOT BROKEN

I AM NOT EASILY DISTRACTED

I AM A SEEKING THE KINGDOM OF
GOD

I AM LIVING A VICTORIOUS LIFE
WITH CHRIST

I AM A WHO GOD SAYS I AM

I AM WALKING BY FAITH

I AM TRUE, LOVELY, INTELLIGENT

I AM THE BEST IN EVERYTHING I DO

I AM AN HEIR OF GOD

I AM WALKING IN MY PURPOSE

I AM FULFILLING DESTINY

I AM BORN AGAIN

I AM BEING TRANSFORMED BY THE RENEWING OF MY MIND TO PROVE THE PERFECT WILL OF GOD

I AM MORE THAN A CONQUEROR THROUGH JESUS CHRIST

I AM NOT LIVE FRUSTRATED

I AM EVERYTHING GOD SAYS I AM

I AM MADE IN THE IMAGE OF GOD

I AM BEAUTIFUL

I AM LOVE

I AM ADORABLE

I AM LIVING A LIFE OF PEACE

I AM A LEADER

I AM A DEVOTED SPOUSE

I AM UNIQUE

I AM BLESSED

I AM WILLING TO CHANGE MY
BEHAVIORS

I AM AM NO LONGER FEELING
DEPRESSED

I AM RECEIVING ALL MY NEEDS MET

I AM INCREASING AND ABOUNDING
IN LOVE

I AM BLESSED WHEN I COME IN, I
AM BLESSED WHEN I GO OUT

I AM INCREASING DAY BY DAY

I AM PRAYING MY DESIRES AND
RECEIVING THEM

Your Daily Affirmations

DECREES TO SPEAK ALOUD ON A DAILY BASIS

I DECREE WEALTH AND RICHES ARE IN MY HOUSE

I DECREE I AM HEALTHY AND IN GOOD HEALTH

I DECREE MY FAMILY IS SET FREE

I DECREE THE JOY OF THE LORD IS MY STRENGTH

I DECREE WHAT GOD HAS FOR ME IS FOR ME AND NO ONE OR NOTHING CAN TAKE IT AWAY

I DECREE I WILL STOP THE THIEF WITH GOD'S WORD SPOKEN OVER ME AND MY FAMILY

I DECREE THE SPIRIT OF GOD IS WITHIN ME

I DECREE I AM LIVING IN GOD'S DIVINE TIMING AND NOT JUST BY TIME

I DECREE I AM LIVING A LONG SATISFIED HAPPY, HEALTHY, PROSPEROUS LIFE THROUGH CHRIST WHICH STRENGTHENS ME

I DECREE MY MIND IS STRONG

I DECREE GOD IS IN CONTROL OF MY LIFE BECAUSE I HAVE GIVEN GOD FULL PERMISSION TO MANIFEST IN ME AT ALL TIMES

I DECREE NOTHING IS IMPOSSIBLE FOR ME

I DECREE NO WEAPON FORMED AGAINST ME SHALL PROSPER OR OVERTAKE ME

I DECREE I WILL REJOICE DAILY

I DECREE I AM JOY

I DECREE I AM SET FREE I AM NO LONGER BOUND BY ANYTHING OR ANYONE

I DECREE I AM JOINT HEIRS WITH CHRIST JESUS

I DECREE THE LORD IS MY LIGHT AND MY SALVATION

I DECREE GREATNESS IS WITHIN ME

I DECREE I WILL NEVER BE SICK ANOTHER DAY IN MY LIFE BECAUSE BY JESUS STRIPES I AM HEALED

I DECREE I AM WHO GOD SAYS I AM

I DECREE I AM CAPABLE

I DECREE I AM STRONG

I DECREE I WILL NEVER STRUGGLE ANOTHER DAY IN MY LIFE NOR MY CHILDREN LIFE

I DECREE I AM READY TO RECEIVE EVERYTHING GOD HAS FOR ME

I DECREE I CAN HANDLE WHAT COMES MY WAY BECAUSE CHRIST IS MY CHIEF CORNERSTONE

*I DECREE EVERY DOOR,
WINDOW, GATE IS OPEN FOR ME*

*I DECREE NO MORE HOLES IN MY
BAGS*

*I DECREE I LIVE UNDER A OPEN
HEAVEN*

*I DECREE THE KINGDOM OF GOD
IS WITHIN ME*

I DECREE I AM BOLD

I DECREE I AM COURAGEOUS

*I DECREE I WILL NOT LIVE WITH
ANXIETY, DEPRESSION OR ANY
MENTAL ILLNESS*

*I DECREE ALL GENERATIONAL
CURSES ARE BROKEN OFF OF ME
AND MY FAMILY*

*I DECREE NO ONE IN MY FAMILY
WILL DIE AHEAD OF TIME DUE TO
SICKNESS OR DISEASE BECAUSE
WE EAT HEALTHY AND WE KNOW
THE PLANS GOD HAS FOR US WE
ARE COVERED BY THE BLOOD OF
JESUS AND WE ARE PROTECTED*

FROM THE THIEF AND THIS WORLD SYSTEM

Your Daily Decrees

Conclusion

It's my prayer that you receive this impartation about "Words Carry Power" into your life. I want you to start to speak life with your words because once you start to make a conscious effort to change your words this will start to change your mindset. This is the principle we are going after. Continue saying what God says and allow your faith to develop. Let's all strive to be imitators of God.

I'm a firm believer, God speaks to us in several ways, through pictures, people, movies, music, and with words we read. We need to see it through our imagination and our words in order for it to come to pass.

Let's be aware of the words we speak because we will have what we say. Words play a huge part of our lives more than you could have ever imagined. Without speaking correctly and spiritually the words we speak have no bearing whatsoever in our lives. We can choose to speak negatively and live as the world lives but it's my responsibility to share what God had imparted to me to give to you. I pray something I have written resonates with your spirit and causes you to change your words you speak daily. The Holy Spirit will recall these words I have written for you when you need them the most.

Scripture says: *"Jesus was matter-of-fact: "Embrace this God-life. Really embrace it, and* *nothing will be too much for you. This mountain, for instance: Just say, 'Go jump in the lake'—no shuffling or hemming and hawing—and it's as good as done. That's why I urge you to pray for absolutely everything, ranging from small to large. Include everything as you embrace this God-life, and you'll get God's everything. And when you assume the posture of prayer, remember that it's not all asking. If you have anything against someone, forgive—only then will your heavenly Father be inclined to also wipe your slate clean of sins."* **Mark 11:22-25 MSG**

We were never intended to speak anything and it will not come to pass. Stop saying you don't have enough money to do something. Stop saying you don't have (whatever you typically say). Whatever you are saying, speak life to your words and watch them come to pass and you will live a happy healthy lifestyle the way God originally intended.

Remember **scripture** says: *"Jesus replied, "Have faith in God [constantly]. I assure you and most solemnly say to you, whoever says to this mountain, 'Be lifted up and thrown into the sea!' and does not doubt in his heart [in God's unlimited power], but believes that what he says is going to take place, it will be done for him [in accordance with God's will]. For this reason I am telling you, whatever things you ask for in prayer [in accordance with God's will], believe [with confident trust] that you have received them, and they will be given to* *you."* **Mark 11:22-24 AMP**

I encourage you to keep a journal and start writing out your goals. Do this daily so you will be able to see them come to pass. Start to speak your words out loud. Remember faith comes by hearing and hearing by the word of God. Something happens when you read aloud. You hear the words you are saying and faith comes by hearing and hearing by the word of God.

Scripture: *"Now faith brings our hopes into reality and becomes the foundation needed to acquire the things we long for. It is all the evidence required to prove what is still unseen. This testimony of faith is what previous generations were commended for."***Hebrews 11:1-2 TPT**

When you speak things into the atmosphere, God hears you and things start to move. You definitely want to be aware and more conscious of the words you are speaking. As you start to speak your words out loud, watch how fast God moves on your behalf, especially when you mix the words with faith and scripture.

My favorite scripture, is a perfect example **scripture**: *"And a certain woman, which had an issue of blood twelve years, and had suffered many things of many physicians, and had spent all that she had, and was nothing bettered, but rather grew worse, when she had heard of Jesus, came in the press behind, and touched his garment. For she said, If I may touch but his clothes, I shall be whole. And straightway* *the fountain of her blood was dried up; and she felt in her body that she was healed of that plague. And Jesus, immediately knowing in himself that virtue had gone out of him, turned him about in the press, and said, Who touched my clothes? And his disciples said unto him, Thou seest the multitude thronging thee, and sayest thou, Who touched me? And he looked round about to see her that had done this thing. But the woman fearing and trembling, knowing what was done in her, came and fell down before him, and told him all the truth. And he said unto her, Daughter, thy faith hath made thee whole; go in peace, and be whole of thy plague." **Mark 5:25-34 KJV**

You then start to put a demand on

your words and speak like the King inside of you "*DECREE*" a thing and it shall be established.

Scripture: "You will also decide and decree a thing, and it will be established for you; And the light [of God's favor] will shine upon your ways." *Job 22:28 AMP*

Here is a different perspective (different translation)

Scripture: ""*You'll take delight in God, the Mighty One, and look to him joyfully, boldly. You'll pray to him and he'll listen; he'll help you do what you've promised. You'll decide what you want and it will happen; your life will be bathed in light. To those who feel low you'll say, 'Chin up! Be brave!' and God will save them. Yes, even the guilty will escape, escape through God's grace in your life.*""*Job 22:26-30*

MSG

Keep in mind when you speak the word of God it will come to pass because the word of God will not return void but it will accomplish just what it was intended to do.

Scripture *"so shall my word be that goeth forth out of my mouth: it shall not return unto me void, but it shall accomplish that which I please, and it shall prosper in the thing whereto I sent it."***Isaiah 55:11 KJV***

Lastly, begin to say positive blessings of encouragement and protection over yourself, family and others.

Words carry power. Speak words of faith.

About The Author

Sharron Downs has a BS in Psychology, Sharron also holds the following Certificates: Best Practices of Leadership, Life Coach, Clinical and Accountability Coaching, an APA certification.

Sharron has several certifications in Healthcare: Medical Technician, CNA, and HCA while Concentrating in the areas of behavioral health, Alzheimer's, Dementia, Parkinson's, Diabetes, PTSD, Downs Syndrome and Kidney Disease.

Sharron is a woman of faith and serves as a keynote speaker and motivator in several spheres of influence. Sharron is a risk-taker, passionate and a motivated self-starter. Sharron has a podcast

"Sharron Daily Inspirations" on all major platforms where you listen to podcasts.

Sharron has a passion to help those suffering from mental instabilities like depression, loneliness, low self esteem, trauma, lifestyle triggers, substance dependence and difficulty with expressing feelings and other life situations.

Sharron also provides support and assistance to elderly patients suffering from dementia, Alzheimer's and those on hospice.

Sharron is passionate about helping leaders thrive in their careers God's way. Sharron has a proven track record in recruitment and retention, training and development, succession planning, mediation, conflict resolution, executive coaching and leadership development.

Sharron has written and independently published over twenty three books all written and inspired by God. Author Sharron Downs is available on Kindle and Amazon.

To purchase these books in bulk for your organization contact via email: sharron@sharrondowns.info

Books:
"Change Your World With Words -Add Value To Every Area Of Your Life"
ISBN-13 9798725146905
ASIN B08ZD6TK8T

"21 Strategies To Overcome Mental Instability: With The Words You Speak"
ISBN-13 9798728031918
ASIN B08ZW3186N

"Beauty For Ashes Book 1 (3 Book Series) - 21 Day Devotional"
ISBN-13 9798731480451
ASIN B091GN7271

"Beauty For Ashes Devotional: Discover Your Value" (Beauty for Ashes Devotional: 7 Day Devotional)
ISBN-13 9798732724219
ASIN B091J98QV8

"Joy and Gladness" (Beauty For Ashes Devotional: 7 Day Devotional)
ISBN-13 9798732804287
ASIN B091NPVTD8

"Renew Restore Refresh: 27 Day
Devotional"
Paperback: ISBN-139798733179094
ASIN B0924CY24W
Hardcover: ISBN-139798480794342
ASIN B09GRHT9X6

"Decree A Thing: Speak And
Command Change"
Paperback: ISBN-139798509544644
ASIN B095GP9HNP
Hardcover: ISBN-139798480008562
ASIN B09GJJCV5

"Dominate Emotional Instabilities:
Break Free- Gain Control of your
mind"
Paperback: ISBN-139798516343889
ASIN B096LPS1Q5
Hardcover: ISBN-139798480720471
ASIN B09GQJMX62

"Beauty For Ashes: 30 Day Journal"

Paperback: ISBN-139798512556382
ASIN B096LYJWR6
Hardcover: ISBN-1397984799998591
ASIN B09GJV9NLB

"Change Your World With Your
Words second Edition"
ISBN-139798510183726
ASIN B095MKPHFF

"Words Carry Power: Speak Words
of Faith" ISBN-13 9798320978697

"Overcome Life Circumstances:
With The Word of God"
Paperback: ISBN-139798532214026
ASIN: B098GSPB75
Hardcover: ISBN-139798480006995
ASIN: B09GJS7RXH

"Beauty For Ashes 21 Day
Devotional"
Paperback: ISBN-139798779713337

ASIN: B09MYYXG2B
Hardcover: ISBN-139798779720625
ASIN: B09MYWXZZS

"Caring, Caregiving and Caregivers:
the look into the elders care plan"
Paperback: ISBN-139798779852050
ASIN: B09MZ1DF6M
Hardcover: ISBN-139798779861854
ASIN: B09MYXXCSP

"Journal for families and caregivers"
Paperback: ISBN-139798792701854
ASIN: B09P4MDQ8H
Hardcover: ISBN-139798792712843
ASIN: B09P5BNGNB

"I'm Not Ready to Say Goodbye...
Coping With Grief: Self Pace Grief
and Personal Journal"
Paperback: ISBN-13:9798815366886
ASIN: B09ZRFDZM

"Revitalize Your Faith in 90 Days"
Paperback:ISBN-139798838311863
ASIN: B0B56YZF13
Hardcover: ISBN-139798838317032
ASIN:B0B4KHFMT4

"Daily Reminder: Get Things
Accomplished- End
Procrastination"
Paperback: ASIN: B0BYLRVQPB
Hardcover: ASIN: B0BY9PYJCX

"Decrees and Declarations : Speak
Powerful Bold Words, Dominate
Your Atmosphere" Paperback:
ISBN-13979-8398889703 ASIN:
B0C87QRNNT

"The promises from God: It's time to
make them personal" Paperback:
ISBN-13979-8859904051 ASIN:
B0CH2FQ6C1 Hardcover:
ISBN-13979-8859327560 ASIN:
B0CGL3ZG2T

"Twenty-One Strategies To
Overcome Mental Instability: With
The Words You Speak"
ISBN-13 979-8865881391
ASIN B0CM3MQDD9

"The Divine Set Up" paperback:
ISBN-13979-8866663934 ASIN:
B0CMQG6HXP Hardcover: ISBN-13
979-8866675470 ASIN
B0CMQJWD8L

"I'm Not Ready to Say Goodbye…
Coping With Grief Journal: Dealing
with Grief " Paperback ASIN:
B0CR4CTXJ8

"People Wake Up: Start living.. Stop
just existing". Paperback: ISBN:
9798879831351

Journal Notes

ISBN: 9798320978697

Imprint: Independently published

www.ingramcontent.com/pod-product-compliance
Lightning Source LLC
Chambersburg PA
CBHW051754250726
48659CB00001B/414